Marvin

A Greenville Legend

David Boyd Lee

Amazon

Contents

Chapter 1

Dedication Page

This book is dedicated to anybody that has ever stopped to pick Marvin up and given him a ride to his next destination.

A portion of the proceeds from this book will go towards a special project at Elm Street Park to honor Marvin.

Chapter 2

Prologue

David Lee

I f you are reading this book, Marvin Jarman has probably touched your life in one way or another. Maybe you were an athlete or the parent of an athlete and he was a fixture on the sidelines or bench at a J.H. Rose ballgame. He has been walking the sidelines at football games, keeping stats at basketball games, or half asleep but still watching a baseball game from the dugout for forty plus years.

Or maybe you know him as a member of the Greenville Recreation and Parks Department family. He has kept beloved Elm Street Park spotless since 1969.

Maybe you have seen him walking down the street and given him a ride to wherever he was headed. That has become a Greenville tradition over the years.

Or maybe you remember him at a Greenville Little League game holding court with RV, Coach Phillips, Dr. Grimsley and the crew up on the hill at Elm Street.

My first vivid memory of Marvin was on the tennis courts at Elm Street Park. My buddy Scott Davis and I would go play out there whenever we could. This was probably in the early 1980s.

One day we were in the middle of a point and I went back for a lob near the fence and almost ran into Marvin. He was picking up a piece of paper that had blown up inside the fence. It might have been the only piece of trash on the ground in the whole park.

He said hello to me. He gave Scott a wave and went on about his business. We called the point a "do over" and went back to playing. Marvin's presence was a part of Elm Street in our world. It wasn't weird at all to two teenage boys that he was inside the fence picking up trash while we were playing.

Years later, Marvin was the free throw coach for Coach Jim Brewington when I played basketball at Rose High. He would chart everybody's free throws during the game, sit between Coach Brewington and Coach Dennis Gibson on the bench, and listen to everything going on in the huddle. It was always good having him with the team in a comforting way if that makes any sense.

Most practices ended with Marvin shooting a free throw. If he made it, practice would be over. If he missed, we ran more suicides. He was pretty clutch with those free throws from what I remember and even if he missed it just gave us a chance to give him some grief. Nobody really cared if we had to run some more. It was Marvin. He was a part of the team.

Most of my married life has been spent in Wilson, North Carolina. My wife Dana and I have two boys named Hunter and Mason who played just about any sport they could get their hands on much like I did back in the day. Both of them played soccer, basketball and baseball for Wilson Fike High School. Fortunately, Fike and Rose started back playing baseball against each during Hunter's sophomore year and they also played some soccer and basketball games against each other.

These matchups might not have meant much to anybody else but they were special to my dad and me. Watching Hunter and Mason compete against my alma mater meant a little extra to us especially in baseball. The reason these matchups meant a little something extra to us was obviously playing against a Ronald Vincent coached team and both of our relationships with him, but even more importantly, Marvin. I wanted Marvin to see my boys play and my dad wanted Marvin to see his grandsons play. To us, it was a rite of passage.

Before each baseball game right after infield was taken, Marvin would come out of the Rose dugout and slowly make his way over to the Fike dugout and find Hunter or Mason. He would shake their hand, ask about me or dad, and tell them good luck. They started to look forward to it after it happened a couple of times. It also made them feel special which is one of Marvin's many special gifts that you will read about in many of the stories in this book.

Mason's senior year Fike played Rose in basketball in Greenville. It was one of those early season ugly basketball games that happened every year. Neither team had figured anything out at that point and time. Rose won by about five or so and it seemed that Mason spent a lot of time knocked down on the floor or double teamed and trapped because he was the point guard. It was frustrating and I could tell he was a little put off when the game ended, but here is the beauty of Marvin.

As the teams were shaking hands in a line after the game, I watched Marvin coming from the Rose side in the back of the line and Mason coming from the Fike side in the back of the line towards each other. When they got to each other, Marvin kind of pulled Mason in a little closer than the rest of the handshakes he had just been giving out and said just a little something to him. Mason's demeanor instantly changed.

To this day, he doesn't know or remember what Marvin said to him. It doesn't really matter. He made Mason feel better. It is just what Marvin does and Mason experienced it and he is better off for it. I'm not sure you can put it into words or I would really try.

When I decided to do this book on Marvin, I didn't want it to be the same old autobiography type of book. You know the kind. Marvin was born in Greenville. Marvin graduated from Rose High. Marvin worked at Greenville Recreation and Parks Department for his whole career. Blah, blah, blah.

I felt like there needed to be a way to better show what kind of person Marvin is. I mean he is the most well known person from Greenville for a reason. And then one day while driving to work, it hit me. Everybody has a favorite Marvin story. Why not let them tell it?

So after deciding what kind of book I wanted to write about Marvin, I went over to Greenville to eat with the lunch crew at Cubbies.

After catching up for a little while, Ronald Vincent, better known as RV, said, "David, tell Marvin why you are here."

I said, "Marvin, I am going to write a book about you. Is that okay?"

He looked over at me and in that Marvin voice said, "Yeah. Yeah."

I said, "I'm going to let your friends tell stories about you. Is that fine with you if they do that?"

He said, "Yeah. Yeah. Somebody already tried to write a book about me. It didn't work out."

And then he went back to eating his cheeseburger. It was so Marvin.

This book is a collection of stories told by family, friends, co-workers and people that love and admire Marvin. Some of these stories are funny. Some of them are extraordinary and some of them will tug at your heart strings, but they are all Marvin.

When I began this book, I thought it would be just amazing, funny stories about Marvin, but it immediately turned into much more about Greenville's favorite son. I just hope you can feel the love for Marvin by every one of the folks that took the time to share with me in the words on these pages as I could hear in their voices.

He is truly a special, one of a kind person. After all, he is the legend of Greenville for a reason.

Chapter 3

Boyd Lee

Greenville Parks and Recreation
Department Director 1967-2007

I started to work for Greenville Recreation and Parks in 1967. One of the first people I got to know was Marvin Jarman because he came down to Elm Street Park every day from Rose High School and my office was located in the little building beside the baseball field.

The longer I knew him the more I came to realize what an exceptional person he was. He was limited in his abilities yet, he was very smart and remembered facts and figures about history, sports and people. I thought he was incredible.

In 1969, I became director and shortly thereafter, Marvin graduated from Rose High School. I had heard through the grapevine that he was probably going to have to go to the shelter workshop.

I knew how much he loved being at Elm Street and Little League Baseball. I also knew that he attended baseball, football, and basketball practices and games every day at Rose High. If he had to go to the shelter workshop, it would totally destroy his every day routine that he loved so much.

So, I decided to call his mom and see if she would be in agreement with me to offer him a full time, part time job with our department in the parks division. I called her and explained what I wanted to do and she immediately broke down crying on the phone. She said her prayers had been answered because Marvin wouldn't have to go to the sheltered workshop which was the place folks with handicaps went to work every day when they were of age. If this could happen, he wouldn't have to go there and he could continue with his daily routine that he loved so much.

So, Marvin was the first person I hired after becoming director and he stayed loyal for my entire forty year career while practically never missing a day of work and always doing whatever was asked of him.

On Marvin's first day of work, I immediately sent him down to the parks division to work. Well, that lasted one day. The first thing they tried to show him how to do was mow grass. He had to push the mower in a line but when he got to the end of the line he couldn't figure out how to swing it around and come back the other way. Instead, he would pick up the mower and had the blade flying all around. They didn't want him to get hurt and he couldn't figure out how to do it the other way.

We immediately realized that with his mobility and the pace that he moved about that this was not going to work. So we decided to give him one responsibility that he could do each day. We assigned him to his love which was Elm Street Park and the task of cleaning the park of trash each day. He took on this responsibility and has never looked back. He has kept the park clean and in perfect condition for his entire career.

We only had one problem with Marvin during his years with the department. We found out he was coming to work before daybreak.

He was worried that he couldn't get the trashed picked up whenever there was a lot of activity the night before at the ball field because he was getting off work at twelve o'clock the next day.

I explained to him that he must wait until the sun came up before he come to work, because we were afraid he might run into somebody in the dark before day break came and we didn't want him to get hurt.

So, he adjusted his schedule to get all his work done between eight and twelve each day. And he worked that schedule faithfully all those years to make sure that Elm Street was clean.

And that is the story of how Marvin came about working at Elm Street for Greenville Parks and Recreation.

He was the first and best hire I ever made.

Chapter 4

Ronald Vincent

J.H. Rose High School Class of 1965

Everybody knows how loyal Marvin is to Rose High Athletics.

You know how much he gets into Rose football. He wears his football gear everyday during the season. Sweatshirts, t-shirts, hoodies. The day football is over? We lose out on Friday night in the playoffs and he will have his Rose basketball stuff on Saturday morning.

He hates losing but will put it behind him as soon as the season is over. Once basketball loses out, he will have his Rose baseball stuff on the next day until baseball is over. When the season is over, he will then go to his Greenville Recreation and Parks Department stuff. It is like clockwork.

He hasn't missed a Rose High football game since 1972 or a Rose High basketball game since 1966. It's like 1275 straight games or something like that.

It is just amazing.

Chapter 5

Griff Garner

J.H. Rose High School Class of 1975

As I thought through my long term relationship with Marvin and of course, it starts with my dad and my family all the way through my grandkids. I kind of wrap it all into Marvin in his own special way over time knows how to be a real friend. He has befriended so many people and that's why people love him so much.

I mean I call Marvin a friend and my kids call Marvin a friend and now, my grandkids want to call him a friend as they get to know him even though they are pretty young. And that's why I love him so much.

Despite being so close and so friendly, he also speaks the truth. In a real friendship you need to be able to speak the truth.

I remember one instance after Elm Street Park was destroyed by Hurricane Floyd they had to bring a group of groundskeepers in to fix it. I think Chris Ball was one of them and he was working at one of the minor league ballparks. He brought a team in and they rebuilt the Elm Street field and made it look immaculate.

The first game back after it had been renovated was on a Sunday and my youngest son Gray played for Optimist. They played in the first game that opened the field back up. Well, Gray was ten and Optimist was the visiting team and Gray was the lead off batter, so he was the first batter to hit on the newly renovated Elm Street Park field.

He played for Marion Crisp and Mitch Jones. Marion was the head coach and he coached first base. So, Gray leads off and I can't remember what team it was against because it was one from the other league and hits a line drive over the first baseman's head into right field.

He rounded first and Marion wasn't sure if he should go to second or not and then he waved Gray on after he had kind of stopped. Sure enough, the right fielder threw him out at second base.

The next day on Monday, I saw Marvin at lunch and I said, "Marvin, do you know who got the first hit at the newly renovated Elm Street Park?"

Marvin replied, "Gray did. And he also made the first out."

He spoke the truth and brought me back to earth when I was bragging about my son getting the first hit.

Chapter 6

Randy Phillips
J.H. Rose High School Class of 1971

One of the funniest stories about Marvin happened at Elm Street Park. I worked with the Greenville Parks and Recreation Department for about twenty years running Small Fry and Big Fry. That's what we called the 5-8 year old leagues. I would teach them from the mound. We would have a ball.

Well, Marvin worked down at Elm Street too. He would come in early and make sure the park was cleaned up and looking good. The big thing for Marvin was his snack about mid-morning and a plan for lunch.

On this particular morning, I told Marvin we were going to Venter's Grill at quarter til 12. Back in the day, Venter's Grill had the best country cooking anywhere in eastern North Carolina, but the thing about going there it was hard to get a seat if you weren't there early enough.

You sat wherever you could. You might be sitting beside the mayor. You might end up sitting with the guy who changed your oil or a doctor or a professor from ECU. You just fell into a chair. It didn't matter because the food was so good. Marvin loved the cheese biscuits and vegetables. Their vegetables were the best.

Marvin would finish his work around the park and then usually walk out on the field about 11 o'clock to umpire the rest of the last game of the day. Now, Marvin would get most of his calls right. I am not saying he got all of them right, but he would do a pretty good job. Plus, everybody loved having him out there.

This particular day the visiting team was winning by one and the home team was coming to bat. Now, the worst thing that can happen in one of these games is extra innings. Nobody wants that because it is easily another forty minutes to play another inning or two.

Now, keep in mind, these are five and six year old kids. Nobody knows what is going to happen. Well, the first two batters get out and we are looking pretty good. The next batter hits one and it goes between about five player's legs. The little boy makes it to first base.

So, now we have a situation. It's about 11:40 and I see Marvin looking at his watch in the field.

Sure enough, the next batter hits one hard and goes between about eleven player's legs. They finally get a hold of the ball and throw it in to second base. Now, the little boy on first base had forgotten to run when his teammate hit the ball so he had a slow start to second.

He takes off for second and the throw from the outfield is coming in. We don't know if he is going to make and here comes Marvin across the field to make the call. Don't forget it is now about 11:43 and we are supposed to leave for Venter's at 11:45.

Now, I'm not going to tell you the boy was safe. He looked safe to me from the mound.

Well, here comes Marvin across the field clapping his hands like he does before a big call. I think he is going to call him safe and they are going to score and we are going to play another thirty minutes.

Marvin looks at his watch and knows he has two minutes to get to my car for lunch. He pegs the rascal out, walks right out the gate up the hill and is standing by my car at 11:45.

Venter's Grill had a lot to do with that team losing that day. I swear that boy was safe. Marvin is a piece of work.

He is the only one that could have done that and gotten away with it.

Chapter 7

Ron Butler

J.H. Rose High School Class of 1980

The one thing that I would like to say about Marvin may shock some people. When I was serving my five years on the Board Of Directors for the North Carolina High School Athletic Association, the first time I came home after a meeting, Marvin started asking me some questions about some of the issues we had discussed and voted on.

At first, I thought he might be kind of joking. No, he was serious.

And do you know what? Marvin probably asked me more good questions during my five years on the board than anybody else.

So, for the next three or four years when it came time to vote on an issue, I would say to myself, "How am I going to explain this vote to Marvin?"

It got to the point if I couldn't explain why I voted a certain way to Marvin then I shouldn't be voting that way.

Chapter 8

Joe Deloach
J.H. Rose High School Class of 1989

When I get asked where I'm from, I proudly tell them Greenville. After we get through the whole Greenville, North Carolina or Greenville, South Carolina thing, they want to know where I went to school.

As soon as I say Rose High, they immediately ask, "Hey, who is that guy? I think his name is Marvin." Everybody knows him.

Greenville is known for three things. B's Barbecue, baseball, and Marvin. And not necessarily in that order.

He is Greenville.

Chapter 9

Brian Weingartz

Greenville Little League Commissioner
1999- Present

About three or four years ago, Rose baseball is making a pretty good run through the playoffs. Each day at about 10 o'clock in the morning, Marvin and I would go to one of the local convenience stores and he would get a couple of Diet Mountain Dews and some sort of snack.

He would change it up. He would get a honey bun, a Danish or a pack of nabs. Well, he got on a roll about halfway through the base-ball season and started getting an oatmeal cookie. Rose was winning and he kept getting an oatmeal cookie every day because Marvin does not eat chocolate at all.

Well, after a while, I noticed he was getting an oatmeal cookie every day. And I told him, "You know Marvin, Rose has not lost since you started buying these oatmeal cookies. You might need to keep buying these cookies, you know?"

And he agreed with me. You could tell it was kind of going through his mind already. He was definitely thinking that.

Well, the manager of the store got wind that these oatmeal cookies were important to Marvin. Then one day, he told me that the corporate office had sent out a memo saying that the store would not be offering these oatmeal cookies anymore. Rose had a month left in the season so this was going to be a problem. Marvin needed his oatmeal cookies.

So, we knew they were going to be running out and we went in one morning and there was one oatmeal cookie left. Marvin got the last one. I asked him, "Marvin, what are we going to do now? The cookies are gone."

He just kind of shrugged it off and said, "We will figure something out."

The next day we came in the store and the girl behind the counter had gotten into Marvin's everyday routine over the last month. Marvin went up to the counter with his Diet Mountain Dews and whatever new snack he had picked out.

She reached under the counter and brought out a whole box of the oatmeal cookies. She had taken all the oatmeal cookies they had left and boxed them up for Marvin.

Each day after that, she would pull his oatmeal cookie out of the box during Rose High's playoff run and make sure he got his cookie. So, I always thought it was funny that she took the time to do that for him.

He was the only one going to their stores that could still get an oatmeal cookie.

Chapter 10

Bill Twine

J.H. Rose High School Class of 1967

We are riding back from a Rose High game. Marvin is riding with us and it's late. We're kind of hungry and the only place we see open to eat is McDonald's.

We go inside and place our orders. Marvin is the last to place his order. Now, if you know Marvin, he is not too keen about fast food.

Cubbie's is fine, but Mickie D's? He is not a big fan, so he is just standing there staring at the menu boards behind the counter.

Someone says, "Marvin, it's McDonald's. They've got burgers and fries."

Finally, he looks at the cashier and says, "Okay, I want a cheeseburger.......no cheese." We were all puzzled.

"Marvin, why don't you just order a hamburger?"

He goes, "I just don't like the way their hamburgers taste." And that was the end of that.

Of course, even though he was the last to order, his food came out first. Always.

Only Marvin......

Chapter 11

Scott "Scooter" Rogers

Voice of ECU Baseball and Greenville Little League

Have you ever been around him when his cell phone rings? It sounds like a tornado warning going off.

Every time it happens in the press box at Elm Street we all get down on the floor and under the cabinets. And he says it is the alarm going off every time it rings.

Half the time it is a telemarketer when he answers the phone. He will answer it and say hello about fifteen times.

It is the funniest thing in the world watching him answer that phone especially when a telemarketer is on the other end.

Chapter 12

Walt Mercer

Marvin's friend since 1999

T he greatest thing about getting to know Marvin is he is the absolute best person for kids to be around. I moved to Greenville 21 years ago and my first child was born 21 years ago. All three of my children have grown up around Marvin.

They have been around him their whole lives. He is the perfect role model and keeps the children straight too. He will also get on them if he needs to.

One day years ago, we were in the back yard and several kids from the neighborhood and mine were around and jumping on the trampoline.

We had one rule about the trampoline. The rule is that only two people can be on it at a time. And, of course, you know there was always one kid that was the odd one out and had to wait their turn.

Well, this one day one of the kids was tired of waiting. They came over to us and complained that is was their turn and the others wouldn't let them have their turn. You know how kids are.

I explained that only two people were allowed on the trampoline again and their turn would be in a minute.

Marvin turns around and says, "A rule is a rule." And that settled it.

We use that even today. If somebody says something or complains, we just say "A rule is a rule. You know what Marvin said."

That's something my children will carry with them the rest of their life. They have heard it all their life and that's the way it is.

How do you argue with that?

Chapter 13

Clay Medlin

J.H. Rose High School Class of 2002

This story about Marvin is just the funniest to me. Rose had a baseball game against West Carteret at Guy Smith Stadium and Marvin was coming to the game. He was walking to the stadium from his house.

Brooks Jernigan was the coach at West Carteret at the time. In fact, he still is the coach there. This particular year, he pulls up to a stoplight in town and sees Marvin walking. Now, he has known Marvin for 30 years. They are good friends and everything.

Now, of course, he opens the bus door and calls out, "Marvin, how you doing? It's hot. Come on and hop on the bus and we will give you a ride to the stadium."

Marvin looked at him just as serious as he could and said, "I can't ride with you. You are the enemy today. I can't ride with you."

So, Brooks laughs, offers again, gets turned down again and finally says okay, and heads to Guy Smith. They pulled in and Brooks comes over to RV and myself and tells us they saw Marvin and offered him a ride but he wouldn't get on the bus.

Well, Marvin apparently didn't get a ride that day and he walked all the way to the stadium from his house. About 45 minutes later,

Marvin shows up all hot and sweaty. It was really hot that day. He is dragging and obviously exhausted.

He walks right in the gate and goes straight to Brooks to shake his hand.

"How you doing? How is everything going?" Marvin does his usual greeting he does with all the coaches.

Brooks says, "Marvin, why wouldn't you ride with me? We've been friends forever. You are killing me."

He is just giving it to him and Marvin repeats that he was the enemy for the day.

Now, Ronald is on it and says, "He isn't the enemy man. You've known him forever. He is good people."

Marvin just looked at him and kind of shook his head like he does.

"Yeah, but what are ya'll going to say if I got off their bus. Ya'll going to think I like them better than ya'll. That's what people say about me sometimes."

And to be honest, Marvin was right. That's exactly what we would have done. He walked miles in the heat instead of giving us a chance to pick on him.

Smart guy.

Chapter 14

Ronald Vincent

2022 inductee into J.H. Rose Athletic Hall of Fame

The first baseball thing that come to mind is when we would play in these Easter Tournaments we always let Marvin call the flip for home team. And he loses probably 90% of the time. Anytime, you know we are getting ready to play one of those games, we just go ahead and get our bats.

One year, we were playing an away game and the scoreboard was broke. He was in the dugout asleep. Knocked out. Well, it got about the third or fourth inning and nobody knew the score.

Marvin wakes up and says, "It is 6-5 in the bottom of the fourth."

I go up to the press box and ask about the score and inning and the young man keeping the books says, "It's 6-5 in the bottom of the fourth."

I went back to the dugout and said, "Marvin, how do you know the score? You have been asleep the whole game."

He just looked at me and said, "It's just the score."

And went back to sleep.

Chapter 15

Ron Butler

2009 Inductee into J.H. Rose Athletic Hall of Fame

The amazing thing about Marvin is he cannot tell a lie. I used to joke that I was going to have Marvin call parents back to talk about their child's playing time.

You know how every parent thinks their child is the best player on the team? I was going have Marvin call them back and tell them the truth.

Can't you hear him? "No, your son isn't that good." He seriously cannot tell a lie.

I used to feed him different stuff and see how he would tell the truth.

"Hey Marvin, I'm probably the best football player to ever play at Rose High, right?"

He would think it over for a second and say, "Well, um, well, maybe wrestling, but you know football. You were one of the good ones, but I ain't going to say the best."

He will just not lie when you feed it to him. No matter what you do, he will not lie.

Chapter 16

Macon Moye

J.H. Rose High School Class of 1975

I'm 64 years old now and Marvin is still a part of my life. I don't get back to Greenville as much as I would like to but when I do I call Ronald and tell him I'm coming.

We will try and do lunch or just go sit at Elm Street Park and marvel what that has become. I don't have to ask if Marvin is going to be able to come. He is always there. He is a piece of everything we do together.

Everybody wants to talk about what a legend Marvin is and what a great person he is, but he has been the same ever since I've known him. He hasn't even changed a little bit, right? He just hasn't.

I told Ronald recently when I was in Greenville that I couldn't imagine going through life and never being upset with anybody. I've never seen Marvin mad with anybody. What a great way to live!

You know maybe Marvin has it all figured out. He may be the only normal person out there and the rest of us are all screwed up. I'm thinking we all need to be introduced to Marvinville because it makes a lot more sense and it's a lot more peaceful to live in his world than ours.

I've got a son and two daughters now and when they were

younger I would tell them about growing up in Greenville. And I would always tell them about Marvin because he was a big part of my growing up. You can't separate growing up in Greenville and being a baseball player and Marvin not be a piece of it.

Marvin is the greatest ambassador Greenville could have ever have wished for because he is consistent. There is never any surprise. You always know what you are going to get. And it is so refreshing.

I told my kids about the presidents thing and they got a chance to meet Marvin. They started asking Marvin questions and he got everyone of them right. They looked at me like they thought I had been making this up.

The greatest thing about Marvin is you don't need to make anything up. The real facts about Marvin is all you ever really need to know.

Everybody should be so lucky to grow up with a Marvin influence in their life. I am an addiction counselor now and I deal with drug addicts and alcoholics everyday and we work on gratitude. We try and turn them away from the negative in their lives and focus what they are grateful for in their lives.

Think about Marvin? I'm so grateful that I know somebody like Marvin and that world he lives in. As I said before, it's got to be the one of the greatest places in the world to live.

I hope people realize what a treasure he is. Ronald certainly understands it. Your dad understands it. Charlie, Ronald's brother, understood it.

He has never had to ask for anything because people want to do for him. I mean he starts out walking somewhere and he is ten steps into it and he will have a ride going somewhere. People will go out of their way to give Marvin a ride even if they are going somewhere different. They just put their trip off and take care of Marvin.

Chapter 17

Howard Vainright
J.H. Rose High School Class of 1976

W hen I was a sophomore at Rose in 1973-74, I was the equipment manager for RV and the baseball team. I went to practices, games, and travelled with the team. As you probably already know, Marvin supposedly has a photogenic memory and remembers everything he reads.

On bus trips I used to drill Marvin on sports trivia. Occasionally, I would have a sports almanac and would ask him questions from it like "who was the winning pitcher in the third game of the 1962 World Series?" It was always some crazy trivia or statistic.

Marvin would think on it for a few seconds, and always come up with the correct answer. Even when we didn't have a way to check his answer, you knew, if he gave an answer, he was right.

His memory is amazing.

Chapter 18

Darrell Harrison

Former ACC football referee of 24 years

I think it is fantastic that there is going to be a book about Marvin and I just want to be sure that there are a couple of stories about Marvin's heart and what a caring person he is. Here are my two examples.

My brother was the head football coach at Wake Forest Rolesville in Wake Forest. It is now back to Wake Forest High School and he got cancer at a young age and ended up passing at 45 years old. And Marvin would see him along with thousands of others at the coaches clinic every year.

During the time that my brother was sick, Marvin never saw me in Greenville without asking, "How was Rock doing?" Except he couldn't say "Rock". It would come out as "Wock".

The thing was he would not ask me and just keep walking. He would stop, look me in the eye and want to know how my brother was doing. It just meant the world to me that you could tell how sincere he was about it.

And then if you fast forward to the last four or five years, my wife now has dementia. It's been a pretty rough go for the last couple of years. She has had it for about five years, and I never see Marvin although I don't see him as often with the pandemic going on, without him asking, "How is Sandy doing?"

And again, he will generally stop what he is doing and he really wants to know how she is doing. And only after I give the report that it is a struggle and we're doing the best we can with the Good Lord's help, he will kind of nod and pat me on the back and then we will get onto sports and how the games are going.

So, that's my two brief stories on just what a great heart he has. And what a great person he is.

Everybody loves Marvin and there are thousands of stories about him. I don't know how there are all going to fit into one book but I sure hope the book will be able to show what a good and caring person he is.

He just has such a good heart.

Chapter 19

Steve Warner

Employee of Greenville Recreation and Parks Department 1992-2021

The Human Resource Specialist called me. She said they needed an employee evaluation for a Marvin Jarman. And they asked me if he was one of your employees.

I said yes, he has been one of our employees since August 18th, 1969. I just happened to have all of our parks employee's information in front of me. It was evaluation time so I was pretty up to date on everybody's start date and info.

I asked her, "Y'all don't have any evaluations on him?"

She answered , "No, we don't have anything on record for Mr. Jarman, but we need an evaluation."

I told her I would call her back and called Deborah at Jaycee Park.

"Do we have an employee evaluation on Marvin on record?"

Deborah asked, "Who is asking for that? Is it the new girls in HR?"

Apparently, they had some new faces in HR and were going through a transitional period. They were getting their new system in place and Marvin's name had come up on their radar.

Deborah told me to do what they asked or Marvin wasn't going to get a cost of living increase. This was in 2008. Somehow, Marvin hadn't gotten an evaluation over the last 39 years.

I printed out the paperwork and went down to Elm Street Park to find Marvin. Only, I couldn't find him.

I went in the Little League office and asked Brian Weingarts if he knew where Marvin was.

Brian said, "I think he went to the store with RV. They should be back anytime."

I said, "Okay, I will wait on them."

"What do you have to wait for? Do you need me to tell him something?"

"No, I've got to do an employee evaluation on Marvin."

Brian just busted out laughing. "Do what? An evaluation on Marvin? He comes to the park. Cleans up. Goes home. That's his evaluation." Brian was being sarcastic.

"Well, I got to do an evaluation on Marvin. This is what HR wants."

About that time Marvin and RV show up, I told RV he might be able to help me.

"I've got to do an employee evaluation on Marvin." And RV had the same reaction that Brian had. He busted out laughing.

Now, when Marvin gets a little nervous or has a little pressure on him, he usually starts kind of grunting and talking to himself. He wasn't sure about this at all.

I said, "Guys, y'all have to help me with this. This isn't me. HR is requesting it. Can you help me? I've got some notes here already that I want to talk to you about it. We can start from there."

And they all agreed. So, we started in on the evaluation.

I've still got the notes from our talk. These are all from the HR incentives and stuff they wanted.

Question #1: What specific job performance area has the employee performed best? Please list specific examples in the last 12 months.

My answer: Marvin continues to provide the service of litter collection at Elm Street Park. Marvin is always at the park completing litter collection on a daily basis. If you don't see him at Elm Street Park in the morning, he is either sick or on vacation. He is very friendly to patrons and deals well with reporting litter issues in the park.

Question #2: Are there any specific job performance areas in which the employee may need further development or training to improve his or her knowledge, skills, and abilities.

I stated this answer as plain as day.

My answer: Marvin needs to continue to understand about the operations of the alarm systems at Elm Street Center. Understanding the procedures would reduce calls. The number of false alarms to the facility depends on his efforts.

We had so many false alarm calls at Elm Street Center that Greenville PD just stopped charging us for them. Marvin had his routine. He would go to work. He would go to the Little League room. He'd go to the vending machine. And then he would go to the bathroom.

The whole time the alarm hadn't been reset and he wouldn't realize it until the PD knocked on the door and Marvin would be in there. It was a silent alarm, so he never heard it.

I don't think he ever met that performance goal in all the years he was here. Sometimes we would have to send staff down there before he got to work to turn the alarm system off. He never got the reward of setting it off. He just heard the PD knocking on the door. So, that was an improvement plan for the fiscal year.

Here was the hardest question I had to ask during the evaluation.

Question: What is the employee's self-improvement objectives for the next 12 months?

Marvin's answer: To continue to do a good job with parks and recreation department at Elm Street Park.

I only did it because HR wanted a copy for their records to justify what he was receiving. This was 2008 and he got the same evaluation in 2013.

I remember sitting there on the bleachers at Elm Street doing this with him and how uncomfortable he was. He didn't want to talk about it. I was uncomfortable and didn't want to talk about it either but we had to do it.

Here is the summary of the evaluation: Marvin is an above average employee and provides the department with positive exposure at Elm Street. Marvin is friendly to patrons and is always looking out for problems on the grounds. Patrons visiting the park in the mornings can always depend on Marvin handling any litter issues.

I tell you. It was awkward. What do you do? Do you grade him on any of these competencies? Work attitude? He has the best attitude ever.

You really going to put unsatisfactorily for any of those initiatives? Give me a break. You can't put unsatisfactory for anything on Marvin. That would be like the ultimate sin.

You would either go to hell or go to jail for the rest of your life.

Chapter 20

Ronald Vincent

2014 Inductee of the NCHSAA Sports Hall of Fame

Another time we went to an Orioles and Yankees game. Clyde King was the Yankees manager.

We were sitting there before the game and the team was warming up on the field and we hear, "Marvin Jarman, what are you doing here?"

Thousands of people are already in the stands and Clyde King spots Marvin and yells at him to come down and talk to him. He asked Marvin if he brought him a barbecue sandwich from Parker's.

Of course, Marvin said, "No."

There are hundreds of people Clyde King has to talk to before games and he picks Marvin out of the crowd. It was unbelievable.

We asked Marvin how he knew him. Marvin said, "I've talked to him before."

He said it like it wasn't any big deal. It was just the New York Yankees manager!

Chapter 21

Joe Deloach

J.H. Rose High School Class of 1989

I played baseball, I coached baseball, and I went to Rose, but then I also worked for the Greenville Recreation and Parks Department too. So, I felt like I had probably more exposure to Marvin than most folks especially when I was working baseball at Elm Street.

Every morning it was me, Randy Phillips, Grant Jarman, Pat Joyner, and Brian Wille. We ran the Small Fry and Big Fry programs. And Marvin worked at Elm Street, so he was a part of our morning drill.

He was just amazing. Yeah, people always want to talk about their favorite Marvin story, but for me, it was just more of a long term thing like spending a lot of time with him. There are a ton of stories and a ton of funny things, but for me, it is just a culmination of how great a person he is.

Loyalty was a big thing for him, you know? Commitment? He was very dependable.

RV likes to say you could set your watch by Marvin.

Chapter 22

Randy Phillips
J.H. Rose High School Class of 1971

One of my favorite stories about Marvin is years ago we went to the Coach's Conference in Greensboro. We had a group that went just about every year. We would stay the whole week and Marvin really looked forward to that time of year like it was Christmas. It was his favorite week of the year.

He got to see all the coaches from around the state and everybody knew Marvin. I mean you couldn't give him any better of a time. He knew everybody. He knew Charlie Adams who was president of the North Carolina High School Athletic Association and he knew just about every coach in the state. It was fellowship time. It was just one big family.

At night, all the coaches from Pitt County would get together in somebody's room and tell stories. We would watch a baseball game, order some pizzas and some of the guys would have a few drinks. Now, keep in mind, this was 25 or 30 years ago.

Well, one night we were all in the room. It was probably about 10 or 15 coaches from Pitt County. We got to asking Marvin questions about sports and everything. Well, you know how Marvin is. He remembers everything about every sport there is.

Well, Marvin is a Yankee man. He loves the Yankees. He could tell you who won the batting title in 1927 or who won the World Series in 1930. It didn't matter to Marvin. He just put it out there. He is like a walking encyclopedia.

Well, low and behold, one of the coaches in the room was a Pittsburgh Pirate fan. Marvin doesn't hate the Pirates, but he is a Yankees man. Marvin doesn't hate anybody.

Well, this coach thought he knew everything about the Pirates and he keeps firing Pirate questions at Marvin. It gets deep in the evening and he is trying his best to stump Marvin. He asks Marvin a question from way back in the day. Marvin frowned and started muttering to himself.

The coach thinks he has him. He thinks he has stumped Marvin! The coach was almost yelling that he has finally got Marvin. And then all of a sudden, Marvin gave him the answer.

Well, the coach jumped up and said, "I got him. I got him." He confidently said Marvin had given him the wrong answer.

It got even later in the night and Marvin was over there in the corner of the room mumbling to himself. "I ain't wrong. I ain't wrong." It was tearing his nerves up.

We got back to our room and Marvin is still tore up. He is walking back and forth in our room mumbling to himself. "I ain't wrong. I ain't wrong."

Ronald told him to go to bed. It took him about two hours to settle down. All you could hear was saying, "I ain't wrong. I ain't wrong."

The next morning we got up and got ready to go downstairs and you could tell Marvin was still perplexed. He was upset. He told me and RV again, "I ain't wrong. I ain't wrong."

Well, about three or four blocks away, I had seen the Guilford County Library when we were driving in. I told Marvin to come on and we would figure this thing out.

We pulled in there and Marvin and I went into the library. I told the lady at the desk what we were looking for and she directed us to a section. We found a book with a lot of lists about baseball history.

Marvin sat down and went through that book til he found the right answer. And guess what? Marvin was right!

I gave the librarian my driver's license so we could take the book with us. We took the book back to the Convention Center. Marvin was going to find that coach out of the 1200 coaches that were there. We found the coach and Marvin had his finger on the page where the correct answer was.

He walked up to the coach in the middle of a crowd, pointed at the book, and said, "I was right."

He slammed the book shut, turned around and walked out of the exhibit hall. That is all he told the guy. In other words, you don't fool Marvin Jarman!

After that, he was just as calm. He had to prove to that guy he was right. And then, we took the book back to the library so I could get my license.

It was just about the funniest thing I have ever seen.

Chapter 23

Beverly Garrett

Greenville Recreation and Parks
Department 1984-2008

I had just started working for the Greenville Recreation and Parks Department. I had met Marvin, but I really didn't know him like I would get to over the years.

I was coming back from lunch and stopped at the light at the corner of Charles and Greenville Boulevard.

All of a sudden my passenger door opened and Marvin got in. He said he needed a ride to Elm Street. I was floored, but gave him a ride.

We've been friends ever since.

Chapter 24

Ron Butler

2009 Inductee into J.H. Rose High Athletic Hall of Fame

M arvin used to stand on the back of the blocking sled when I was in school. He did it when my brother was there and did it when I came though. Well, 40 or 45 years ago, Marvin was a little heavier than he is now.

One day, RV pulled us aside and told us, "Look guys, Marvin needs to lose a little bit of weight. Y'all need to quit picking him up. He needs to walk places. He needs some exercise."

So, it was kind of tough when you would be driving down the road and you'd see Marvin up ahead. You had to act like you didn't see him.

Do you know how hard it is to drive by Marvin standing on the side of the road when he knows you see him? The look of disappointment on Marvin's face was hard to take.

We did that for little while, but it didn't last long.

Chapter 25

Clay Medlin

J.H. Rose High School Athletic Director
2014- Present

Probably seven or eight years ago, I got an IPhone. We're sitting out at Guy Smith Stadium and we're checking out my new phone. I am telling the guys all the stuff it does and Marvin is sitting there listening. He still had a flip phone at the time.

I told him it was a smart phone. He kind of laughed when I called it a smart phone. I told him it had the internet, email, text messages, and it would do just about anything a computer would do.

He said, "Let me see that thing." I give it to him and he is holding it and looking it over.

So I tell him, "Marvin, that phone will tell you anything you want to know in the world. You can find anything out in the world."

He is just staring at the phone for about thirty seconds and we are starting to get a good laugh about him inspecting that "smart phone" so hard.

He finally holds the phone up to his mouth and says, "Who is going to win the World Series this year?"

Now, we are really laughing and I said, "Marvin, it can't predict the future. It can tell you everything that has happened in the past."

He looked kind of confused and said, "Why do I need to know what happened in the past? I already know all that."

I said, "Who won the World Series in 1947." He spits out the answer almost immediately. Guess what? He was right.

He already knows what happened in the past. He was wanting to know who was going to win the World Series that year.

Chapter 26

Walt Mercer

Marvin's friend since 1999

I don't remember why they went, but Ronald and Marvin went down to the Atlanta area for some function. They stopped by Lou and Ted King's house to visit and eat dinner.

Lou's sister Ramona lives next door to Marvin and when he goes over there, Ramona will cook a big spread for supper. She is a really good cook.

Well, Lou knows Marvin eats over there all the time and she also knows Ramona is a great cook. So, she is feeling the pressure to put on a big spread because Marvin was coming to dinner. She makes this big dinner, they all sit down to eat, and it was really good.

After the meal was over, Marvin is sitting there looking around and it looks like he isn't satisfied.

Somebody says, "Marvin, what's wrong?"

And he says, "Well, Ramona always fixes dessert." It just killed the whole thing.

Lou's dinner was great, but Marvin was looking dessert.

Chapter 27

Ronald Vincent
J.H. Rose High School Class of 1965

I will tell you what, he will move mountains to get to a ballgame. One time we went up to St. Louis for a major league game. Several of us went and our tickets the second day were in the upper deck.

Well, Marvin does not like heights. We didn't know that. We are sitting there and they play the national anthem and he won't stand up. He knows he is supposed to, but he is holding onto the arm rests as tight as he can.

Well, we sit back down and he was getting to be alright until the helicopter comes. It's a television helicopter and it was actually below where we were sitting we were so high up. Well, Marvin got up and left.

Later, we look down there on the third base dugout side in the first row sat Marvin.

We asked him, "Marvin, how in the world did you get there?" He said, "You just walk down there and sit." That's Marvin.

Another year, East Carolina was playing Temple in Philadelphia in football and the Orioles were playing the Phillies in World Series and a group with Marvin went up there. Same story.

They decided to go by the baseball game. They don't have tickets, but Marvin walks right in the front gate and got a seat about two rows behind the first base dugout during the World Series.

I wasn't there, but Mitchell Jones was at the game and goes to the bathroom and there's Marvin Jarman.

He said, "I've been all around the world and I didn't ever think I'd run into Marvin at the World Series in Philadelphia."

Chapter 28

Brian Weingartz

Greenville Little League Commissioner
1999- present

The North Carolina Prep News would put out a yearbook that had all every team's info and their football schedule in the state. I do not know how it started and I don't know how Marvin got his hands on one at the beginning, but Marvin loved that thing. It is usually published sometime around mid-July in time for the coaches convention. It was a big thing for Marvin when he got his copy.

For years, he would have to wait for the coaches convention to get his copy and then he figured out you could order ahead of time. I don't know how he figured that out. He must have read it somewhere.

On June 1st of the year he figured this out, he walked into my office with a blank check and his signature on it and handed it to me. And said two words, "Football book."

I told him I did not think you could order it early but he insisted you could. I did some checking around and actually called the lady who published it because he wouldn't leave me alone about it. This was before email.

She tells me that you can order them early. All you had to do was send a check to this particular address and decide how many you wanted and you would get them in the mail. We did this for years.

You never had to remind him and without fail, he would walk into my office with that blank check and say, "Football book." And he would have his book by about June 10th. It was a big day for him.

Well, one year, Randy Phillips and the guys were giving him a hard time that they had gotten their books and Marvin hadn't gotten his. Well, he was a wreck for about two hours trying to figure out why they had gotten their books and he had not gotten his.

The truth was they didn't have their books either. That happened every year until he figured out they did not have a book either.

Anyway, he would get his books every year. He would get three or four of them. He would have one in my office, one at home, and maybe one at Rose High. He had them stashed all over the place and would study those things. He was always reading them. It was such a big deal when those books would arrive.

Well, one year, the books were taking forever to come. He would usually get them by the 14th or 15th of June and all these days are passing and the books aren't showing up. Time keeps passing and it is like mid-July and he is all to pieces.

He wants me to call, so I called the lady. It is a Friday afternoon and she answers and tells me that she had some issues getting them together that year but they had just arrived in a big shipment at the post office in Charlotte. She lived out in the country and she said she would probably get over there to pick them up in the next two or three days.

So, I asked her if she could possible make sure that the first batch she sent out to make sure that Marvin Jarman in Greenville got his books. I told her how important those books were to him. She agreed to do send him his books as soon as possible.

Marvin could not understand how she could know the books were in and it was going to take her two or three days to pick them up. It really worried him.

After that year, the books did not get printed for about three years. I think the lady was the caregiver for her parents and didn't have the time to get them together. For those years, we went on the internet and printed out all the schedules so Marvin could have them and study them.

Anyway, Marvin found out this year they were going to start printing the book and it was like Christmas to him. He was so excited. I kid you not that the book sits in my office and the first thing he does when he gets to my office is to grab that book and read it every day. It means the world to him.

It's something I've shared with him and it is very neat to see how much that book means to him. And he is like clockwork on June 1st with that blank check. When he found out they were publishing it again, on June 1st he was standing in my office with that check. "Football book."

He didn't forget even three years later. It's just amazing.

Chapter 29

Ted King

J.H. Rose High School Class of 1980

My wife Lou and I left Greenville in 1985. About three or four years later, we were back in town visiting and we were driving down Elm Street. We see Marvin walking down the street.

I said, "Hey, there's Marvin. I am going to stop and talk with him."

She looked at me and said, "He isn't going to remember you. We've been gone too long."

I laughed at her and said, "Ok. Watch."

So, I drive up to him and roll down the window. He pokes his head in the window and says, "Hey, Lou. Hey Ted."

He not only remembered my name, but he remembered my wife's name too. The memory that guy has is incredible.

She was blown away.

Chapter 30

Scott Davis

J.H. Rose High School Class of 1987

My story with Marvin goes back to growing up in Greenville in the seventies and eighties. Playing sports in Greenville Marvin was just a constant. Our coaches would change. Our teachers would change and maybe your friends may change a little, but Marvin was a constant. He was always the constant for us. He was just a settling influence on our group.

Even though Marvin was involved in a lot of sports, most of my personal memories were on the baseball field. One of my earliest memories was RV would get his eye on some younger players when they were in Little League and start working with them. He would pick us up in his truck on a Saturday morning and we would jump in the back and Marvin would be with him in the cab.

We would get our own private coaching session with RV and then we would go to McDonald's or somewhere to eat. You and I did that all the time with RV. And that is where I probably first got to know Marvin on those Saturday workout sessions.

Marvin was even there when you weren't playing sports. You would see him while you were driving around town and pick him up.

He was just such a constant like I said earlier for us kids in a world that was changing pretty fast.

My personal favorite Marvin story happened my senior year at baseball. The end of basketball season went a little long because of the playoffs, so there was an overlap for Marvin with the start of baseball practice. Seeing that Marvin was the free throw coach for the basketball team, he decided to go to the basketball playoff game instead of the first baseball practice of the year. So, he missed practice.

Well, Marvin shows up for the second practice of the year and RV is waiting on him. RV calls the whole team up and lines us up on the left field line.

"I've got a dilemma on my hands. I need your help figuring out what to do, because we have strict rules on this team. If you don't practice, you don't dress out and you certainly don't travel with the team. I don't know how I can hold my players to a higher standard than I hold my own coaches."

You could see Marvin getting a little bit disturbed. He was picking up on what RV was laying down. And then RV really started laying it on thick. I mean it is a best friend's job to give his friend grief whenever he can. We all knew what was going on.

"I don't know what to do about this situation. So, I am going to leave it up to you guys and you guys are going to decide whether Marvin is going to travel with us to our next game."

We are all still lined up on the left field line and RV lays it on a little thicker.

"I am going to count to three and if you think Marvin should travel with us you just need to take one step forward." And he was really methodical about it.

"One." Maybe two guys stepped forward. And he paused for a little bit.

"Two." Maybe one more guy stepped forward. And he paused again for a little bit.

So now, of course, the whole team is in on RV busting Marvin's chops and almost everybody is still standing firmly on the left field line. Marvin starts shaking his head and kicking at the dirt like he does. And then he just throws his hands up like he wants RV to stop before saying "three".

Now, everybody knew Marvin always had a big pack of Juicy Fruit in his pocket back in the day. And he never needed the Juicy Fruit more than he did at that moment. He goes down the line of the guys still standing on the left field line and hands everyone of them a piece of gum.

RV goes nuts. "Aw, come on man. You're tampering with the jury. You can't be doing that."

At this point the whole team is falling out laughing and the joke was over. We had such a good time laughing with him and it started our season off in a great way.

And again, RV is doing his job as Marvin's best friend to poke fun and give him a little ribbing. Needless to say, Marvin travelled with us to the game.

There a couple of things that I love about that story. One, it shows the incredible relationship that Marvin and RV have. And two, Marvin is obviously such a good sport but a bunch of teenagers just spent some time with Marvin and walked away with a smile on their faces and piece of gum in their mouths.

And I think that is just about how ever interaction I had with Marvin growing up ended. With a smile and a piece of Juicy Fruit.

Chapter 31

Bill Twine

J.H. Rose High School School Class of 1967

I t is a hot Sunday afternoon and I'm a bit bored so I check the Babe Ruth schedule and see there are a couple of games scheduled at Guy Smith Stadium. I got there about the time the first game was finishing up.

The few spectators that are there are still sitting along the top row. That is where you can catch the best breeze. It is the usual suspects; RV, Joe Davis, Dr. Jimmie Grimsley, Marvin, and his antagonist, Randy Phillips.

Unfortunately, on this hot, humid June afternoon there is little if any breeze. So, it is hot.

Randy is aggravating Marvin as usual and keeping him from his Sunday afternoon nap. Marvin has had just about enough of Randy's mouth about the time the scorekeeper comes over to ask RV a question.

As he starts to leave, Marvin asks him if he can sit in the press box for the second game. The press box is air conditioned and Randy won't be in there. Marvin has this all figured out.

The scorekeeper says sure, but you have to help me with the PA system or the scoreboard. Marvin tells him he doesn't know how to run the scoreboard.

"The PA system it is then," says the scorekeeper.

The second game is a Senior Babe Ruth game and these tend to pretty laid back affairs. Marvin's first duty is to announce the starting lineups.

First of all, he goes through the home team which is all Greenville guys and he does okay since he has known all the players since they were five years old. But the visiting team have a few players whose names aren't exactly eastern North Carolina.

Marvin gets through the first few okay and then comes the Italian kid.

"In weft (left) field, number 8, John Smith. At third base, number 22, Joe Pizz...oh my gosh."

He goes on and runs into another tough one.

"In wight (right) field, number 14 ...., Oh lord, must be Joe's brother."

It was the greatest lineup announcement in Guy Smith Stadium history.

On this Sunday, the visiting team looks like they had a tough time getting nine players together to play. The second baseman is a rather small kid who looks about 12 or 13 years old. Senior Babe Ruth is for 16-18 years old, but it is okay. It is Senior Babe Ruth, it's a hot Sunday, and the boys just want to play ball.

And, of course, the first ball hit is a sharp grounder at the second baseman and it goes right between his legs. This is repeated several times during the game. The ball is either just out of his reach or hops over his glove. It just isn't his day.

The game is getting out of hand and nearing its conclusion. Finally, the beleaguered second baseman gets a routine hop and makes the catch and throw to first.

From the PA, which accidently was left on, we hear, "It's a mirable (miracle)."

At which point, the top row can be seen falling out with laughter.

Chapter 32

Griff Garner

Member of 1975 J.H. Rose High Baseball State Champions

Another thing about Marvin is he is willing to invest time and energy into a friendship which reminds me of a story my wife Christy told me one time. I grew up in Greenville and Christy moved here in ninth grade and she met Marvin when she got over to Rose High.

Well, she worked for Greenville Parks and Recreation at Tot Lot down at Elm Street Park between her sophomore and junior years at Rose. That's where she really got to know Marvin better and they became friends.

The next summer she went to work for Little Mint at their Green Street location across the Tar River Bridge. It was somewhere over there near that Harris Supermarket.

When she saw Marvin one day she told him, "Why don't you come visit me? I don't get to see you anymore."

Sure enough, one day not long after that, Marvin came walking in the door to eat lunch with her. He had walked all the way across town and across the Tar River Bridge to eat lunch with her.

He invested the time and energy at her invitation to be a good friend.

Chapter 33

Ron Butler

2009 Inductee into J.H. Rose High Athletic Hall of Fame

In Pitt County, everybody knows Marvin. That's not a shock to anybody. A few years ago, he was at Professor O'Cools eating and I'm leaving and he asked me where was I going.

"What's up Marvin? Where do you need to go?"

"Baseball game."

"Come on. I will give you a ride."

We pulled up to the gate and I was ready to explain to everybody that I was just dropping him off. With him in the passenger seat, they just waved us on. I got so close to the ticket booth I could have touched the tickets. I've never been treated like such a VIP until I had Marvin in the passenger seat.

Everybody knows him. And as soon as they saw Marvin, they just waved us on in. It's amazing.

Chapter 34

Chip Harrell

Greenville Recreation and Parks
Department 1976-2009

T hrough all the years, and that's a lot of years, I have never met a more courageous, personable, friendly, polite, generous, courteous, reliable, honest, sincere, trustworthy, likable, thoughtful, modest, kind, unassuming, positive, gentle and just genuinely great man than Marvin Jarman. He is the legend and Mr. School Spirit.

His visits to Jaycee Park everyday were always the highlight of the day for all us ladies in the office. He always brightened our day.

Chapter 35

Scott "Scooter" Rogers
Voice of ECU Baseball and Greenville Little League

T he first story I think of when it comes to Marvin is actually back when I was playing Little League. It was during RV's baseball camp. You know how Marvin always stands out in the field and umpires.

We were at Perkins Field and I hit one up the middle into center field and I actually got thrown out at first base by the center fielder. Marvin made the call.

Now, the center fielder was Hunter Christopher who went on to play at Rose and in college, but I still got all over Marvin's case about it. I told him it was 11:45 and he was just ready to go to lunch and that's why he called me out. I thought of anything I could to just give him the business.

And, of course now, I tell him he did it because it was Hunter Christopher out there and if it benefited him it would benefit Rose, because obviously, his playing ability was a lot better than mine.

To this day whenever we argue about it, he still says he got the call right. We love to give him grief about his umpiring skills, but he will never change his mind on that call.

Chapter 36

Mike Campbell

J.H. Rose High School Class of 1980

We would travel to away baseball games and RV would always drive the bus. The general rule was under-classmen sat in the back of the bus and as each year went on you got to move up towards the front of the bus. So, my junior and senior year I got to sit next to Marvin in the front seat right behind RV.

We always had a bet on how long it was going to take Marvin to fall asleep. Many times he would not even make it out of the city limits before he would be knocked out.

Back in those days, the school buses had those luggage racks in the top of the bus. I'm not sure who it was but I think it was a dude named Junior Neal. Junior was a smaller guy.

This one time Marvin fell asleep as usual and Junior climbed up in those racks and got above Marvin. The buses during those days always had a broom in them to sweep it out after every trip.

He got above Marvin and started tickling his ear with a piece of the broom. Marvin kept swatting it away in his sleep until he finally just leaned over and put his head on my shoulder to finish his nap. He never woke up.

He slept with his mouth open and by the end of the trip I had Marvin's slobber all over the shoulder of my uniform. We laughed the whole time and Marvin never flinched.

He just kept on sleeping. RV watched the whole thing in the mirror just shaking his head.

Chapter 37

Griff Garner

J.H. Rose High School Class of 1975

Marvin graduated with my brother and he knew my dad too, but you know he is friends with everybody regardless of race or gender. He loves athletics but he was friends with non-athletes too.

I have four kids. The two boys played baseball and knew Marvin. I have a daughter who cheered at Rose High, so she knew Marvin well, but we also had a daughter that only danced at the private academy. She was not involved in any athletics. Her name is Ashley, but just like my other three kids she invited Marvin to her wedding. That's how much they all thought of him.

I kind of tie it all up back to friendship. He is a dear friend of mine and my family. I think the good Lord takes someone who may have shortcomings in certain areas and he gives them additional abilities in other areas. I think he gave Marvin an ability to touch people's hearts and to be friends with people and to be loved by people. He has done it for years.

The last thing I will say is Ronald deserves a lot of credit for how well he has treated Marvin. Ronald has lasted so well here in Greenville.

One of the reasons people love Ronald is because of Marvin and one of the reasons people love Marvin is because of Ronald. I may have said that backwards but one of the biggest reasons that people love both of them is because of the other person. It is special to watch them together.

Chapter 38

Ron Butler

J.H. Rose High School Class of 1980

We are at the Coaches Clinic a few years ago and Marvin is hungry. So, I told him to come on and we would go get something to eat. We drive down the road to Biscuitville in Greensboro.

I've taken Marvin quite a few places in Pitt County so it is no surprise to me that everybody knows him. Now, when you are with Marvin, you are with Marvin. He isn't with you, you are with him. It doesn't matter who you are. You are with Marvin.

We walked into Biscuitville in Greensboro, North Carolina and three different people said, "What's up Marvin?"

I was like, "What the heck?"

At home, it wouldn't have surprised me, but we were 165 miles from Greenville.

Everybody knows Marvin.

Chapter 39

Joe Deloach
J.H. Rose High School Class of 1989

They teach you a lot about business life and sales or whatever the case may be that the main thing is how you treat folks. Marvin was the original and the best at this.

Everyone was important. Everybody mattered. He always took the time to speak to you and ask how you were doing. It didn't matter if I had seen him fifteen days in a row. He always asked how I was doing. He always made that effort.

Even now after all these years, we have a daughter in Greenville and we go back for games and that kind of thing. When you see Marvin, you make a point to speak to him.

You stop your car, you stop your conversation with whoever you are talking with, and you go speak to him. He has that status. He is a legend. And so now, I get to introduce him to my kids and that's pretty cool. Then I get to tell the stories to them and go back thirty or forty years.

He was a teacher. The way he treated people probably stuck with me more than anything over time and had a big effect on me. It didn't matter if you were a secretary at a business or the mayor of Greenville he was the same way. He was so genuine. The original.

And that made a big impression on me and I didn't even know it at the time. I make sure I do that with my business and I learned it from Marvin. Not to mention, he was the source of gum for all the young folks.

As college kids, we went and did what college kids do and who knows how much sleep we did or didn't get, but we did show up for work the next day. And looking back, we learned that level of commitment from Marvin.

It didn't matter.to him It could be pouring down rain or six feet of snow on the ground. Marvin was going to be there and so I needed to be there too. And he didn't even have a car.

That's another one of those things I could say "thank you" to him for. We were learning from him and didn't even know it.

Chapter 40

Randy Phillips
J.H. Rose High School Class of 1971

One time we were coming back from Greensboro from the Coach's Convention. This was years after the Guildford Library story. They used to have the East West Football game on Thursday night to finish up the conference.

RV, Marvin and I would usually watch the first half and then get on the road before it got to be too late. Rv was driving that old burgundy station wagon he had and Marvin was sitting in the back seat.

We were driving back one year and it was late. Ronald kept looking in the rearview mirror and said, "Look at that sucker. He is already asleep."

You know how Marvin is. If he rides three feet, he goes to sleep. Well, I told RV I was going to keep him awake. There was no way I was going to let him go to sleep. So, I started firing questions at him.

"All right Marvin, how about if you got married?"

He said, "I don't know about that."

"Let's pretend you got married. I want you to describe your future wife. Tell me what your future wife is going to be like."

"She is going to be pretty."

"Ok, what do you mean by that?"

"She is going be blonde."

"Short hair or long hair?"

"Long. Long hair."

I said, "Okay. Name some of her characteristics."

"She got to know how to cook."

Ronald said, "Do what? He said she had to be a good cook?"

Marvin said it again, "She has to be a good cook."

I said, "Okay, if she is going to be a good cook, what is the first meal she is going to make for you?"

You know what that sucker answered?

"Soup."

We couldn't believe that was his answer. All the meals Marvin loves and he wanted soup.

Ronald said, "What in world are you talking about? Why didn't you say steak or chicken or something like that."

"Had steak yesterday." I thought RV was going to wreck.

"Alright, what kind of job was she going to have?" I was into this conversation now and wanted to see what other kind of plans he had.

We thought he'd say a secretary or a nurse or something like that. Instead, he came back with, "She has to be a teacher."

I said, "You want to marry a teacher? You know they don't make much money."

"That's okay. She has to work at the same school I coach at."

"Whoa. Whoa. She has to work at the same school as you. Why is that?"

'She got to work at Rose High. I will be there."

I said, "So, you wouldn't let her work at Farmville Central or DH Conley?"

"No, she got to work at Rose."

"Alright, what kind of car would ya'll have?"

He answered immediately, "Oldsmobile." I have to admit the man had a plan.

"What color?"

"Green." Would you think there would be any other color?

"Okay. How about your house. One story? Two stories? Three stories?"

"One story."

"One story. Why one story?"

"Don't like stairs." RV was barely keeping the car on the road.

"Alright, one more question Marvin. Where you going live? What city?"

He said, "Are you crazy? Greenville."

He has got it planned out. That is just the way he is. He has a plan. I bet most of us didn't have a plan like that when we got married.

Chapter 41

Mike Campbell

J.H. Rose High School Class of 1980

When I was a sophomore at ECU, RV hooked me up with a job delivering newspapers for a year. We had to meet at the old Pirates Chest on the corner of Charles and Greenville Boulevard at quarter to five every morning seven days a week. Marvin was RV's assistant.

I wasn't living at home then. I had moved out to the country, but Marvin still lived down the street in the same house with his mom at Stratford. It was probably three quarters of a mile walk for Marvin to get to the Pirates Chest.

RV would be there a lot of times because he would be subbing in for another driver because this was a seven days a week job. Do you know Marvin never hardly missed a day? It had to be pouring down rain or he had to be really sick.

And I don't think I ever understood. He was there to help me. I didn't have enough money to pay him or even buy him a Pepsi, but he was always there to help.

I had a little Pontiac Sunbird back then and he was a big guy. I'd put the front seat down and he would get in the back seat.

When we would pick up the papers, he would hand me the

papers from the back and I would wrap the paper in plastic while driving with my knees. He saved me a lot of time. He was a really big help.

On Sundays, it was even harder. The News And Observer Sunday paper was thick.

I'd tell him that I wasn't sure if I had room for him, but we would somehow get him in that back seat and pile the papers in on top of him. When we started all you could see was the top of his head, but after a little while he could start moving his hands again and would hand me the papers.

He never complained. He was helping me.

There were some really cold mornings I thought to myself Marvin is never going to make it and he would be there.

Amazing.

Chapter 42

Bill Twine

Greenville Recreation and Parks
Department 1978-2007

I was practicing with my Little League team at Elm Street Park. Towards the end of practice, I hear this faint "help" off in the distance. I look around, but don't see anyone so I go back to practice.

A few minutes later, I hear "help me". Again, I stop to look around and ask the nearest players to me to see if they heard anything. All I get out of them is some shoulder shrugs. Nope, they hadn't heard anything.

Well, practice end and while we are gathering up the equipment to leave the field, I hear "help me" again. This time it sounds like it is coming from the Elm Street Center.

I looked over to the center, 30 or forty feet away, and I see a shoe, a tennis shoe dangling from a small window by its shoestring. And then I hear that pitiful voice again. "Somebody help me."

I go over to the building. I can't see in the window because it is a small window about eight feet above the ground, but there is the shoe and it looks familiar because of the numerous knots tied in the laces. I only knew one person who ties their shoes in multiple knots like that.

And once again, I hear that pitiful voice again. "Somebody help me."

"Marvin, is that you?"

"Help Bill, help me. I'm wocked in," says the voice.

"Marvin, what are you doing? How did you get locked in?"

"I don't know. I came in to use the rest room and the dumb door locked and I can't get out."

"So, why did you throw your shoe out of the window?" Pretty smart if you think about it.

"I was trying to get somebody's attention."

I checked and sure enough, the door was locked. I tried to talk him through how to unlock the door from the inside but not no avail. Fortunately, I used to have an office at the center, so I thought I still had keys to the building. Unfortunately, I didn't have them with me but I thought they might still be in my car in the parking lot a few hundred feet away.

I told Marvin I was going to go to the car to get my keys.

"Don't leave me. I don't want to die in here."

"I'm not going to leave you Marvin. I'm just going to my car and I will be right back." I left Reid and a couple of players, so they could talk to Marvin and assure him I had not left.

I check my car, find the keys, and get the door unlocked and release Marvin from his prison. We also retrieved his shoe.

On the way up the hill to the parking lot, I asked him, "Marvin, do you need a ride?"

"Yes, Rose High please."

Chapter 43

Ronald Vincent

2014 Inductee of the NCHSSA Sports Hall of Fame

B ack in the day we would be riding down the road in the days before GPS on the school bus going to a game and Marvin would be fast asleep up in the front of the bus. I mean he would be knocked out.

We would come to a stop sign out in the middle of nowhere and be about half lost. We would wake him up.

"Marvin, do we turn here?"

He would look around and say, "No. It's the next one. Next right."

And then he would go back to sleep.

He was always right.

Chapter 44

Ron Butler

J.H. Rose High School Class of 1980

Years ago, Rose had a coach named Lonnie Baker. Coach Baker loved Marvin just like everybody else does. He was picking on Marvin one day.

Marvin told him, "I was here when you got here and I'm going to be here when you're gone."

That is just about as truthful a statement that Marvin could tell anybody.

Coach Baker moved on to another school and Marvin is still at Rose High.

Chapter 45

Walt Mercer

Marvin's friend since 1999

Marvin always has something on his mind or some kind of conflict he is trying to work out. He is at his happiest when Rose High is winning especially state championships. One of us could win the lottery and not be as happy as Marvin when Rose is winning. That's his thing.

I think it was 2006 and we were down in Durham at Wallace Wade Stadium for the game. Rose had just won its fourth straight football championship.

I had rode with RV and Marvin to the game and we were waiting for Marvin to come out after the game. They had all their celebrations and everything and afterwards, he finally made it to the car.

He was so happy that he does his best Dick Vitale impression. "Four in a row, baby." And pumps his fist. He was so happy.

He just loves Rose High.

Chapter 46

Joe Deloach

J.H. Rose High School Class of 1989

I gave Marvin a ton of rides in my car. I don't know if he liked riding in my car necessarily. I didn't have air conditioning and it would be 1000 degrees in August.

He would be sitting over there in my pleather seats and he wouldn't be getting a lot of relief. He probably thought I was crazy, but he didn't turn down that ride.

My sister was a high jumper at Rose. I mean it's not like Marvin was hanging out at the sand pit with all the high jumpers and pole vaulters at the track events. But even today, forty years later when I see him, he always asks about Renee.

It's amazing the memory he has.

Chapter 47

Mike Campbell

J.H. Rose High School Class of 1980

Marvin and his mom moved into our neighborhood at Stratford probably when I was 13 or 14. This was before I got to know RV.

We had a competitive neighborhood with guys like Mike and Roger Williams, Billy Dough and Johnny and Lloyd Jackson. We were always playing something. In those days, we could go across the street to the ECU practice fields and play whatever game we came up with that day.

Marvin would show up and he would have his handkerchief in his pocket. He would use that as his whistle. Now, especially when we would be playing basketball or wiffleball, he would throw that handkerchief on the ground when there was a foul or calling somebody out.

These were the heydays of Billy Martin and Earl Weaver in baseball, so when Marvin made a call we would turn our baseball hat around and get all over Marvin. It was never anything serious and Marvin understood we were just imitating what we had seen on television. We were just playing and Marvin was playing his role as the umpire in the fun.

It was amazing how he went along with us. It was all in fun and then it was nothing when we were done. It was always in fun.

Years later, Ted King and I worked on the ball fields for the recreation department. Will Sanderson, Money Box, and Randy Phillips all worked Small Fry and Big Fry. When it rained, we would meet at the building beside Elm Street Park and play this game we called Jack.

We'd get in that little building with the wiffleball we had in there and go to it. Marvin would be the umpire. Man, the misery he took. It didn't matter what kind of call he made, one of the teams would get on his case.

"Are you blind?"

"That was a terrible call."

We would turn our hats around just like we did when we were over at ECU when we 13 or 14. And Marvin took it so well. He knew we were just playing and he was a part of the show. He was so good.

Man, we did some laughing.

Chapter 48

Clay Medlin

J.H. Rose High School Class of 2002

We were practicing in Zebulon at Mudcats Stadium after we won the Eastern Finals in 2008. We were getting ready to play Aldrick Hill Baseball in the state finals and they had a prominent coach named Hal Bagwell that RV had known for years.

Marvin had a cell phone at the time and he is umpiring a coach pitch scrimmage down the right field line. Now, he doesn't have my number saved into his phone, so I tell RV that I'm going to mess with Marvin.

RV says, "Don't you do it. Don't mess with him."

And I said, "I'm going to do it." So, I went around the corner of the stadium so Marvin couldn't see me and called him. The boys all knew what was going on.

I disguised my voice. "Hey Marvin, this is Hal Bagwell. How are you doing? We are looking forward to seeing you guys this weekend."

Marvin comes back with his usual. "Yeah, yeah, yeah. I heard ya'll pretty good." He loves talking to coaches. It is his favorite thing in the world.

"Yeah, I heard you guys have a nice left handed pitcher?"

Silence. He just quit talking.

"Mark Wilder? Is that the left handed pitcher?"

Now, he is all to pieces. He would not talk. He is walking around throwing his hands in the air like he does.

So, RV yells at him from the mound. "Marvin, who you talking to? What are you doing?" At this point the boys are starting to get a kick out of it. Marvin put the phone down.

"This is Hal Bagwell."

Of course, RV knew it was me on the phone and says, "That's pretty cool. Talk to him."

"He wants to know about our pitcher."

"You can tell him we got a pitcher. Tell him about him."

"Yeah, we got a left handed pitcher." And put the phone back down.

And then I said, "Marvin, I heard you guys have a lot of power in the middle of the order and some speed at the top of the lineup."

He just hangs the phone up on me.

RV said, "Marvin, why did you hang up on Hal?"

"I can't give away our secrets."

Now the boys started in on him, "Marvin, you told him we had a left handed pitcher. You told him we had power in our lineup and speed at the top of the order."

"I didn't tell no secrets. I'd never tell secrets on our team."

About thirty minutes later, I called him back. "Marvin, this is Jason Mills at DH Conley."

"How you doing, Jason?"

"Look, I was talking to Coach Bagwell a little while ago. He called me for a scouting report on you guys. He said he had talked to you and you told him Rose had a left handed pitcher and some power in the lineup."

"Oh, God. No. No. Ronald I need to talk to you."

He walked right on to the pitcher's mound in the middle of practice. The boys are just dying. Everybody is crying laughing.

So, the boys start in on him. "Marvin, did you tell him we had a left-handed pitcher? Did you tell him we had power in our lineup?"

"Jason Mills. Hal Bagwell. Everybody in the state is going to think I'm telling our secrets. I'd never tell our secrets." He was all to pieces.

About that time I came back around the corner and told him it was me.

He just said, "Oh, OK. Alright." And he was good.

Periodically each season, we will do that to him. We will pull out the phone and act like we are the opposing team coach. He will be just as happy as he can be until you ask him a question about the team. "Marvin, do ya'll have a good pitcher?"

"Oh no. I can't talk to you." And he will hang the phone up real quick.

He knows it's me. He knows we are messing with him. But, he still can't get it through his mind that it is okay to talk to them.

Chapter 49

Macon Moye

2008 Inductee into J.H. Rose High Athletic Hall of Fame

I might have spent more time with Ronald than just about anybody in Greenville that played baseball. He used to pick me and my brother up when I was eight or nine years old and I hadn't even got started playing.

I played Little League baseball and he was my coach and then I played high school baseball and he was my coach. We won state championships in Little League and we won a state championship in high school. I've been trying to remember when Marvin became apart of the entourage. It was most certainly in high school.

We had great assistant coaches in Tommy Jordan and Donnie Moye, but Ronald was always in charge and Marvin has always been a piece of whatever happened to me. I was in Greenville a long time and baseball was a large part of it even though I played all sports. Baseball is what I remembered most and Marvin was a major part of that. He was a part of everything we did especially during that state championship run in 1975.

Now, I think everybody knows Marvin has the innate ability to fall asleep in about one minute. He doesn't really care where he is.

You could be in the middle of a conversation with him or riding to a game and that head would get to bobbing up and down.

Ronald would look at us in the mirror of the bus and say, "Marvin is tired. He needs a nap."

Back in the day, we weren't driving nice buses. They were just school buses. We would get a twig or something and tickle his ear. His head would pop up out of a deep sleep and he'd look around and then it would pop back down and fall back asleep. We did this over and over. It was really how we entertained ourselves on those drives to Rocky Mount or Wilson or whatever we were going.

Chapter 50

Ronald Vincent

J.H. Rose High School Class of 1965

O ne story I like to tell is Joe West was calling the World Series one year. We see him at McAlister's in Greenville before it started. We asked him if he could get us tickets and we will fly out there to Philadelphia and go to the World Series. Parker Overton agreed to fly us up there for a game on Tuesday. It was about six of us.

So, I called Joe and he agreed to get us tickets in Philadelphia but suggested that we wait and fly to New York on Thursday and go to Yankee Stadium because you know how good that will be. So, I tell Marvin we aren't going to go Tuesday and we are going to wait until Thursday and go to Yankee Stadium.

Marvin loves the Yankees. He said, "No. No. No. Can't go."

I said, 'What do you mean you can't go? It's Yankee Stadium."

He said, "Javyee football has a game Thursday. I already missed one this year."

We went to Philadelphia.

Chapter 51

Walt Mercer

Marvin's friend since 1999

M arvin is a gem. I am better person for knowing him and my kids are certainly better for knowing him. He is a special person.

Chapter 52

Don Octigon

Director of Greenville Recreation and Parks Department

I knew Marvin as a kid, but I probably didn't really know who Marvin was until middle school. I went to E.B. Aycock and then Rose High School. So, I feel like I have known him forever through just playing baseball and him being around Greenville. I would probably see him at Elm Street Park the most.

As I got older, I probably started to get to know him better as a freshman at Rose. He was at every single baseball game and practice. He would always umpire our scrimmage games which is the story I will share. He was always amazing that he remembered your name, your family's names, and even what you did in a game against a specific opponent last year. By the way, he was never wrong.

As far as Greenville Recreation and Parks, he has worked for our department since like 1968 or 1969 I think. His job was to keep Elm Street Park clean and he gave everything he ever had to his job. He always gave a plus effort, but I will tell you that he also never missed his Diet Mountain Dew and snack mid morning break. He was like clockwork. He would be there at 8:30 and at 12 noon he was ready to go. There is not many people that have been on staff for Greenville Parks even close to that amount of time.

He is just a special guy. He always wants to know how you are doing. How your family is? Those sort of things mean something to him.

When he retired, he kept coming to work at 8:30 in the morning. He just kept showing up and doing his job even though technically he was retired. He would stay at the park until RV picked him up for lunch.

I finally threatened to put him back on payroll because he was working and wasn't getting paid. I'd joke with him about payroll because every Monday he would be cleaning up the park.

And he would say, "No. No. I'm done working." And then he would show up again the next day. Just incredible.

He is also the best umpire RV has at his summer baseball skills camp. He never misses a single summer camp. And he is like the all-time umpire. However, he is the only umpire that can stay in right field down the line, umpire the whole field, never miss a call, and be asleep standing up.

Marvin has slept through many baseball camps at Elm Street and Guy Smith. He would especially struggle in the dry heat in the middle of the summer.

When I was 13 years old and going to camp, I remember Marvin being the umpire and I walked up to him in the middle of a scrimmage and he is dead asleep standing up. I don't know how he does it.

And then later on, we would get on the bus to go to an away game and he would be asleep before we got out of the Rose High parking lot more times than not. He would fall asleep and then wake up at our destination. We couldn't wake him up. I guess he knew exactly how far we had to go to get to the game. And then, he would wake right up when we got there.

Everybody has cool memories like that with Marvin. It's not just me or you. It's everybody. I mean nobody has anything bad to say about Marvin. He has always been a good guy. It seems like he knows everybody in Greenville. And everybody that went through Rose

High. I mean he knows my dad who went to Rose High back in the day.

He is truly missed with our department although really he is still around Elm Street. He and Randy Phillips still run our 6-8 year old camp. Randy and Marvin are still the entertainment. The kids may not know who Marvin is when the camp starts but they sure know him before it is over. Those kids are just another group that are going to have great Marvin memories like the rest of us.

When he retired, it was awesome the amount of people that showed up from everywhere for the retirement party RV and Brian Weingartz put together at Elm Street. People came from all over and they said some of the nicest things about him. The community loves Marvin and Marvin loves the community. It's a pretty cool thing to see.

Think about what all he has seen at Elm Street. All the baseball games. All the tournaments. The expansion. Tennis. Camps. Playgrounds. Picnic shelters. He has seen it all. If he started in 1969 like I think he did, he worked something like 49 years until he retired. That's just incredible.

He has had such a positive impact on so many generations of people. He has meant so much to me personally I don't think I can even explain it. And then you think of the impact he has had on Elm Street and our park system itself? I don't think that can even be measured.

I am glad this book is going to tell some of what he has meant to the Greenville Recreation and Parks Department. Some people may not even know he was a part of our staff for all those years and that part of Marvin's story needs to be told.

To sum it up, he has meant so much to this community and what he has given back to the Greenville community over the years is legendary.

Chapter 53

Mike Campbell

J.H. Rose High School Class of 1980

It's been forty years since I've lived in Greenville. Whenever I see him to this day, he asks about my nephews and my sister. It's just amazing. And he isn't just asking. He really cares.

I think that is the key. Marvin isn't making small talk. He actually cares. We should all learn from that. He isn't just making conversation.

There are going to be a lot of funny stories and everything about Marvin, but I'm telling you since I was 13 or 14 he has always been there. The dedication to friendship is what does it for me. That's what I remember the most.

The funny stories are there. I've got all kinds of those. But him asking about my family forty years later and the newspaper thing.

He is just unbelievable.

Chapter 54

Ron Butler

J.H. Rose High School Class of 1980

I n the 50 years I've known Marvin, I have never walked away from him feeling worse than how I felt walking towards him. You always feel better after you talk to Marvin.

Chapter 55

Braxton Patterson

Wilson City Little League Commissioner
2006-2016

Well, I started working for Wilson Parks and Recreation Department while I was going to Southern Nash High School. I went to East Carolina and was lucky enough to do my internship with Greenville Recreation and Parks and then got hired full-time there not too long after by Mr. Lee. I guess you could say I'm a Parks and Recreation kid.

I think my favorite Marvin story goes back to the beginning of the Highway 264 Challenge between Greenville Little League and Wilson City Little League. But even before that, I vividly remember the first time I ever saw Marvin.

The first time I ever saw Marvin or even knew who he was, he was walking down the side of the road. I was with Dennis Vestal, Ben James, and Dean Foy coming back from downtown Greenville heading back to Boyd Lee Park on Charles Boulevard.

We went past him and either Dennis or Dean were like, "Oh my god, there is Marvin. He is walking by himself on the side of the road. We need to turn around and go pick him up."

Now, I didn't know who he was and they are looking back to see where he was walking while we figured out a place to turn around.

Before we could get turned around, somebody had already magically picked him up and they were like, "Good, someone got him. We just needed to make sure he had a ride."

So, I asked which seems like a stupid question all these years later, "Who is Marvin?"

They gave me a brief history and when I say brief, I mean for the rest of the ride back to the park, of details and stores about Marvin. He is Mr. Rose High School. He works for Greenville Recreation and Parks. They told me all about him and what he means to the community. I thought it was pretty fascinating.

I can't really remember the first time I ever got to speak to Marvin but Dennis told me that the first time I met him he was going to ask me what high school I went to and then tell me some random fact I didn't even know about my own school. And sure enough, Dennis was right. That's exactly what he did.

Years later, after umpiring for Brian Weingartz and working in Greenville, I moved back to Wilson to work for the recreation department and run Wilson City Little League. So, I had gotten to know Marvin a little better.

And then Marvin would come over with Brian or RV whenever Greenville would be playing in a state tournament we were hosting. And I was always happy to sit with them and watch the games when I could.

A couple of years after Wilson City Little League got up and running pretty good, we had the idea to start some kind of way for Greenville and Wilson to play each other and enjoy each others stadiums. So, Brian, yourself, and me got together and came up with the Highway 264 Challenge which turned into the Dr. Jimmie Grimsley Highway 264 Challenge a few years later after Dr. Grimley passed away.

Dr. Grimsley was a huge supporter of Greenville Little League and a big supporter of ours due to his ties to Wilson, so naming it after him made perfect sense.

When we first started, Brian and I would just compare teams and try to make the best matchups for the preseason games. And then, about the time Troy Blaser started as our commissioner, we decided to draw the teams out of hat and do it live on Facebook to add a little to the proceedings.

We also decided to have special guests select the teams from each league. And, of course, Marvin has always been Greenville's special guest.

And so now, the fun is every year right before Thanksgiving we all get to get together and make the selections and talk a little baseball in November which is always nice. When we would pick a team back in the day, we would try to give some history and background on the teams to add a little bit to the broadcast on Facebook for anybody watching.

Every time we would talk for a little to long we would have to wake up Marvin over in the corner of the room and of course, Scooter Rogers and Brian would get a big kick out of that. And then we would all go to lunch which was Marvin's favorite part of the trip.

You know Greenville has always been a dominate Little League program and Wilson is only just around 15 years old but we would win a game or two. We knew how strong Greenville was and how deep their talent pool is so we would be pretty happy with two or three wins.

One year, the challenge finished tied with four wins apiece. Brian and I joked the mythical Dr. Grimsley Trophy was stuck in Greene County for the year.

Anyway, I think it was in 2017, Wilson actually won our first Highway 264 Challenge. And we all decided together that Marvin was to blame because of the way he picked the teams for Greenville. We gave him grief all year. We told him it was all his fault. He just took it stride like he does everything else.

Little League means a lot to both the Greenville and Wilson communities. Greenville has sixty plus years of history behind it and Wilson is over fifteen years now. Both places have great facilities and awesome stadiums. And we both host all kind of tournaments that bring people to our towns. It is just a great setup in both cities. It's pretty special.

Greenville has that great history and hopefully, one day Wilson will have a deep history like Greenville does, but the one thing Wilson will never have is Marvin. He is such a big part of Greenville's history in so many ways.

He is one of a kind.

Chapter 56

Epilogue

David Lee

Thank you to everyone that contributed to this book about Greenville's favorite son. It was so much fun trading stories with old and new friends. The enthusiasm to share their favorite Marvin story with me was evident at the beginning of every phone call and their love for Marvin always ended every phone call.

Yes, Greenville is blessed to have Marvin, but the city is also blessed with some really good folks.

When this book went to press, it hadn't been decided what was going to be done to honor Marvin with a portion of the proceeds of this book. I do know it will be something at Elm Street Park after conversations with Greenville Recreation and Parks Department. We will make sure it is something worthy of Marvin because nobody is more deserving.

Special thanks to everyone who contributed to the contents of this book. It has been an absolute joy putting this book together.

Thank you to RV, Weingartz, Clay and Coach Phillips for their direction, stories, support and overall enthusiasm toward the project.

Thank you to Betsy Rascoe for designing the cover and back of the book. That was pretty cool what you did.

Thank you to Ashley Micelle for the editing and proofreading of the book. A second set of eyes was much needed.

Thank you to my wife Dana for listening to all my ideas, thoughts, and ramblings over the last couple of years about the book. She deserves a medal for putting up with me all these years.

And I can't forget my man Vinny. Thank you to Vince Nelson for taking all those beat downs on the golf course over the years. Vinny, you asked if you were in the book, so there you go.

And last, but definitely not least, thank you to my dad Boyd Lee for having the sense, courage and foresight to hire Marvin all those years ago and to the Greenville Recreation and Parks Department for embracing Marvin into their family for all these years. I spent a lot of time at Elm Street and Jaycee Park during my formative years and the example you guys all set made a big impression on me. Much love to all of you.

And most importantly, thank you to Marvin for being Marvin.

I don't think anything more needs to be said.

Chapter 57

About The Author

D avid Lee is a Greenville, North Carolina native and currently resides in Wilson, North Carolina with his wife Dana. They have two sons, Hunter and Mason. He is a proud graduate of J.H. Rose High School and North Carolina State University. He has been the Director of Parks and Recreation for the City of Wilson for the last twenty years.

David is a past President of the North Carolina Recreation and Parks Association and the 2018 recipient of the prestigious Fellow Award which is the NCRPA's highest honor. He was also a 2011 inductee into the J.H. Rose High School Athletic Hall of Fame and is most proud to be a member of the 1980 Greenville Little League City Champions Jaycees team.

David has been the author of the popular column The Short Side in the NCRPA News magazine for the last 25 years. He also wrote a Saturday column in The Wilson Times for over two years and remains a guest columnist.

His first book titled "Every Moment Counts" is a collection of his columns covering life, work, parenthood, and anything else that came to mind. He avoids columns about marriage which is why he and Dana have remained married for 29 years.

His third book, "Every Moment Counts Second Edition", is scheduled to be released in 2024.

Made in USA - North Chelmsford, MA
76823_9798858734086
02.21.2024 1358